Forever Grateful To You:

Made in the USA
Columbia, SC
05 July 2021

41428074R00061